CW00505284

Kingdom Excellence

1, Volume 1

Joseph Kasonga

Published by Joseph Kasonga, 2023.

KINGDOM EXCELLENCE

First edition. November 7, 2023.

ISBN: 979-8223337607

Written by Joseph Kasonga.

TITLE: KINGDOM EXCELLENCE

Acknowledgment

I thank God for His Word given for this season and for His guidance in writing this book. It is by His grace.

I appreciate Apostle James Mbugua (Fountain Gate Church Nairobi-FGCN), Dr. Lucy Ng'ang'a (FGCN), Pastor Isaac Munuria (FGCN), and Pastor Charles Mutua (Gospel Outreach Church), whose lives and ministry greatly enriched my insight into this topic of excellence.

I appreciate Pastor David Kasonga and Pastor Penninah David (Kingdom Glory Church-Nairobi) for laying out the heavenly pattern of excellence in daily living and ministry. You are highly favored by God.

INTRODUCTION

Excellence is the essence of the highest quality possible. It is the best state of an activity and its result; the Christ-centered disposition of a man's heart concerning work and living. The kingdom of God is the rule of God in and through His sons on earth. Thus, when we talk of kingdom excellence, we are talking of living a life in God which is, high in standards in terms of the way of doing things and the results obtained. Living a life of grace that fully glorifies God and benefits man, living in the fullness of Christ.

In our society today, excellence is like a water drop in the ocean. In most cases where a bit of excellence exists, it's more of human perfection than Godly excellence. A form of social perfectionism because there is less regard to the Word of God. People put in place complex human rules to strictly control and direct others. Enforcement is through laws, organizational regulations, and family practices. The rules enforce a particular behavior code, productivity, and avoidance of the consequences of error in a sensitive environment.

Practicing kingdom excellence means recognizing and adopting the principles of the Word of God necessary for living in heavenly patterns. Instead of imprisoning people, it is a way of liberating people to operate profitably by the grace of God. Challenging believers to live fully as sons of God and thus drawing the patterns of life from Christ.

As world government systems continue failing, the entire humanity is going to look up to the church to provide solutions to challenging global and local issues. The sons of God will have to be manifested on the earth to bring healing and restoration. Their excellence in life will determine how well the earth auto resets itself.

Becoming excellent starts with the realization of the need to operate in a heavenly pattern. Relying on God's grace continually and the constant awareness that whatever you are doing is for God. I hope you will embrace the exhortation to pursue excellence in your life; by looking at the Rock, you were hewn from and conforming to its patterns. I hope to appeal to you by showing the things to let go, the practices to embrace, ultimately pointing you to Christ.

WHY WE NEED EXCELLENCE

Excellence is the quality of an entity or a process that is perfect. Being excellent is having the best disposition of mind and heart concerning how you think, talk, and work. Excellent thinking is the fruit of the mind of Christ. Talking excellence is releasing words of grace. Excellent working is having a style of work that is most productive and is Christ-centered.

People can be termed as excellent in their thinking, speech, and work without regard for God. Such a manner of excellence is incomplete and eventually results in significant error and pride in self. All success draws from Biblical principles.

It was A. W. Tozer, who said that *"we are not in salvation to live a life of peaceful stagnation but one fueled by the original urge for exploits."* Christ is not coming for a church under siege and in need of rescue. He is coming for victorious persons that have distinguished themselves and shown the world how to live.

The world is daily sinking into more profound moral, economic, and social failure. The governments are also running out of solutions with a corresponding increase in apathy towards political systems of governance. There is a need for people who offer working solutions, healings, immunity, and restoration to individuals and systems. Such people can only be those who have seen God and have gotten a unique pattern of living from heaven and not the failing world patterns. They can only be sons of God who have chosen to demonstrate the patterns of perfection from the Father. Kingdom excellence is a demand upon every believer to manifest as a son of God.

"For the earnest expectation of the creation eagerly waits for the revealing of the sons of God. For the creation was subjected to futility, not willingly, but because of Him who subjected it in hope; because the creation itself also will be delivered from the bondage of corruption into the glorious liberty of the children of God" Romans 8:19-21

As sons of God take their place, the earth's systems will automatically restore to the original default state. Where restoration does not happen, there will be a judgment on such erroneous orders. There will be a judgment on churches that are in error, countries, and even world systems such as finance systems, health systems, etc. The only way to live as a son of God is to adopt a living style that is perfected by grace, an extraordinary life free of mediocrity, laziness, and worldliness.

THE KINGDOM OF GOD

"One day, the Pharisees asked Jesus, 'when will this kingdom of God come?' Then Jesus replied, 'the kingdom of God can't be detected by visible signs. You won't be able to say, 'here it is!' Or 'it's over there!' for the kingdom of God is already among you." Luke 17:20-21

The kingdom refers to God's rule in and through His sons over the entire creation. The kingdom has existed from the very beginning and continues to live in the present age to the eternity future. God's rule and power are eternal, and they are everlasting because there is no one else besides Him. The way to understand this matter is by knowing that the kingdom is in operation in two ways. It has come offering men salvation of their souls and dominion over the earth. It will come in full force by subjecting all human authority to Christ's rule.

Through the salvation of God, we have become members of His household. As sons of God, we have a dominion mandate over the earth. The dominion is vested in the image of God in us. It is a mandate that requires us to operate in excellence. In doing it rightly, we will be pursuing the prosperity of the saints. The success of the saints refers to the treasures God releases to his sons freely in Christ. Kingdom treasures include fruitfulness in spiritual living, which is growth and multiplication, a continual increase in the grace of God, victory over self, love, unbroken fellowship with the Holy Spirit, constant worship of God, and wealth (material, divine health, and spiritual).

The rule of God over a believer's life brings transformation and attracts God's blessings as the person walks in obedience. Blessing is God's goodness poured upon a person's life in whatever form He decides to. I realize as I write this book that there is an awakening of the church in Kenya and Africa to what real prosperity entails. After years of suffering from misrepresentation, believers seem eager to understand this matter again. There is the realization that effective ministry requires access to resources.

This book is a step to direct us in the right perspective of life and work in Christ. As we examine excellence, the Lord will progressively reveal to us His nature of excellence, and our eyes will open to see how the Father works. From there, we can set out to do what we see Him doing. The standards of God's kingdom are higher than all human patterns, and the believer should pursue something bigger and better than what the world has to offer. The believer is to live in a divine style that is incomprehensible to the world. No wonder the world cannot understand him for his ways are peculiar to reasoning and human intellect. In this, there is a tragedy that has been when the believer seeks to be recognized by the world. He loses his salt, and the light becomes faint.

FAMILY

"You saw me before I was born. Every day of my life was recorded in your book. Every moment was laid out before a single day had passed."
Psalms 139: 16

All life comes from God. All children are God's blessing. His purpose is for every child to grow under the excellent care of the parents entrusted with the responsibility. Contrary to the myth of unwanted pregnancy and unexpected children, every person should know that before God, it does not just happen. He sanctions that conception by releasing life, His very breath into the young one. Whether born in marriage or out of wedlock, it is a God-given soul.

While conceptions do happen outside of the ideal timeframes and environments, God does not hinder conception in unlikeable circumstances because it is a given privilege to the person. Once a mother conceives a child, there is no question of their validity, only the appreciation of the child as given from heaven. A child's home is the first and the principal place where he or she learns about life and God. Through the expression of family love, care, and mentorship, a child learns a pattern of living to follow. Depending on the nature of upbringing, a person can turn out in many ways. However, not all have had the opportunity to grow in stable families. Some have suffered rejection and abuse in the hands of the very people responsible for them. Others have had no one to call family.

Today we have a better family in Christ. The Almighty God is our Father. He is the Father who never fails, ever faithful, whose love endures through all generations. God releases grace to us for holy living, passion for every good work, and hope for the future. He invites us to prepare our future with Him. Our lives are not cast in stone; they can be made better in God. All we need is to submit to Him, and then He will produce Himself in us. He has revealed Himself to men through Christ. Christ is the image of the invisible God. Whoever desires to know the

9

heavenly Father must look at Christ. In God, there is a better family. We are not to discard our biological families; instead, we are to love them and help incorporate them into the household of God.

While the state of the world will continue to worsen, there is hope for the believer of today and for all who will join God's family because He safeguards His sons during all trouble. The sons must stand firmly in faith, bearing a good conscience for victory.

PATTERNS OF THE YOUTH LIFE

The young person (male and female) today is getting caught up in a web of six wrongs that hinder his path to excellence. They are not the only troubles plaguing his walk, but these listed summarize his limitations.

Lack of patience

Some youth tend to be impatient, whether it is seeking a job, building a business, ministry work, or relationships. The energy of youth runs hot and cannot fit in a single activity; many brilliant ideas that could change the world die at the hands of troubled youth. Many lives spoil at youth.

The young of today (referring to those less than thirty-five years of age) have grown up in rapidly changing environments and technology. These quick changes have cultivated a fast kind of living. Many youths have shifting affections, short attention spans, lots of energy, and desire for instant gratification. Attention is given depending on whether something affects one personally or is entertaining else; it is no bother. The patience to work on something depends on how relevant it seems at sight; not how important it is.

Impatience is synonymous with all age groups, but it bites the hardest in a young life. It is the young who have not yet tasted the bitter fruits of impatience in a big way. And we need not learn from our experiences, and the lessons would be few and unnecessarily painful. We better learn from God, our Maker, and good examples set before us. Impatience is demonstrated by a king who asked, *"Why should I wait for the LORD any longer?"* **2 Kings 6:33**. The king sought to kill Prophet Elisha, just a day before the siege ended. Impatience gnaws at the works of faith, consumes faith, and blinds reason.

In cultivating patience, remember it is God who installed those great desires in your heart. So, wait on Him to fulfill them. Impatience often strikes just before the right thing happens, in the dark period before dawn. Impatience brings embarrassment when the real thing comes into place. Do not embarrass yourself with impatience by regretting things you said or did in haste. Any successful person has a sort of conviction built on priorities, goals, and standards to guide him on short- and long-term basis. That person understands that many things require a process of incubation to mature.

Patience does not imply sitting idly and waiting for things to fall into place; patience involves active waiting. It requires serving, hoping, and exercising faith as you expect. Patience is the time of practice and learning. It is the time a person should prepare for their expectations. If you desire to start a business, it is time to learn all you can learn about startups. Waiting to learn when the opportunity is ready is a recipe for failure.

Patience is a virtue, a fruit of the Holy Spirit's working in the believer. The Spirit of God works in the heart of the believer to produce patience founded on the hope that God will fulfill a desire. The Holy Spirit directs a person's energy to a particular direction, as He moves within the believer imparting peace and joy that clears confusion and brings order.

Lack of lasting Commitment

Commitment involves focusing on a particular course in a way that limits freedom of action in other activities and directing efforts to the selected path consistently. The limit to work elsewhere reduces the millennial's commitment to various endeavors as they would rather be a part of many than in one. Be it spreading the gospel that suddenly becomes too costly and uncomfortable, a fellowship group that feels too strict, a true friendship whose boat is leaking water, an organization that has hit rock bottom in the course of its life. The call for commitment in such situations attracts a frown from people who see it as an attack on individual freedoms.

However, there is hope. Many people have remained connected to a course in the face of trials and served as good examples. They are the people who know no higher price in the pursuit of their stated goals, daily paying the cost for what they believe is the real deal. The commitment of Enoch to God is a worthy example for us today. The man walked with God until he was no more. The commitment of the early church in the face of persecution challenges us to do better. Surprisingly today, we find it easy to commit to workplaces and academics while commitment to God's work is little. A person can wake up at 4 am to prepare for work, but rarely for prayer.

When you love somebody, you want to talk with them often; you want to know them more and more, as in a marriage you give yourself to a partner for better or for worse. Our relationship with God requires more significant commitment than all human relations. Apostle Peter challenges us *to sanctify the Lord God in our hearts*, to set Him as the primary focus of our hearts. Sacrificial loyalty in seeking the kingdom of God rewards eternally. Commitment is a noble thing, so instead of half-hearted devotion to tasks, the Lord Jesus called us first to count the cost. Then if you choose to do something, you do it with all your heart. Complacency must have no portion of our lives we must do the best.

Familiarity weakens our commitment to various tasks too. When you get used to something, you cease to see its significance and begin taking it for granted. You know a person who has gotten used to walking with God loses the passion and the value of the relationship.

God calls us to fan into flames the gifts He has put in us. He requires us to let the fire of the Holy Spirit burn in us continually. In Prophet Isaiah and Apostle John's visions of heaven, we see how the awesomeness of God births in the heavenly beings pure, intense, and unwavering worship. How they continually offer to God worship by all means possible.

We have to continually see the good of what we commit to all through! The God we serve is our Father, and because He knows we are weak humanly, He gives us grace for service. He is the perfection of fathering, far better than our earthly fathers. Our lives should manifest God's unfailing grace. Sons of God, commit yourselves to Godly causes with all your strength. The building blocks of commitment include prudent time management and the consistency of action. To commit is to love. The exact definition of love is commitment.

Culture of reading

Reading is a challenge to many people, not reading or writing per se but doing it beyond the academic or work reasons. One asks, why should I spend days studying a book, magazine when I know all that I need? Why should I buy a Bible when I have a soft copy? Any written stuff which appears hard at first sight cannot get to see the light of day. Satisfied with the information from daily news and friends, some of the young people never seek the real content behind what they receive. A truly successful person is a learner. There is something about reading that opens up the mind wider.

Churning pages is work, but learning makes the difference between the person who knows how to do something well and one who knows why something should be done. In an organization, it is the person who knows why they do the things they do who grow up the levels. The worker who only knows how to do it may remain in the same job level all their life despite their expertise. Moreover, it is well documented that people who know how to do things well are only promoted to their level of incompetence. In other words, they get promoted to the level beyond which they have no requisite competence.

Reading wide provides knowledge, and knowledge is power. In today's society, information is precious. We are in a time when a lot of information is needed to excel in any field. The Bible rightly says that in these times, knowledge will increase. ***"But you, Daniel, keep this prophecy a secret; seal up the book until the time of the end, when many will rush here and there, and knowledge will increase." Daniel 12:4***

The knowledge you have should be relevant to right living, the divine knowledge that edifies. You should only have good knowledge but concerning evil, know nothing. The free seeking of education was a reason for the fall of man in Eden. Adam sought to know as God, instead of desiring to learn to be an exact representation of God on earth. Proper knowledge is helpful for productive work and informed living.

Reading is one way of learning from people's experiences, which you would not get elsewhere. It is a source of encouragement, mentorship, and mental growth. That is why, from the tender age, we read and are supposed to continue the practice throughout life. At a time when getting a good mentor is an uphill task, you should learn from people who have gone ahead of you.

Irrespective of your passion in life, reading is a good thing for us all. Reading suitable materials opens up the mind in a unique way, exposes the person to great ideas, challenges dogmas, and beliefs held by a person. The written words bear the life of the writer's speech, which is released by reading and hearing.

The Bible is full of believers who were good readers, even those who did not write something of their own had something written about them! And what is nobler than to study the Word of God, the Word of life which transforms men to saints. Whether you read other stuff or not, study the Word of God diligently. Hear the Word of God as you read the Bible. The Word is life, builds faith, and releases light to men. The next spiritual revival will be for the Word of God, not signs and wonders, although they will accompany the Word. When the Lord Jesus slept amid a storm in the lake, there is something He knew the disciples did not. He had learned from the Word how to sleep in the storm before speaking to the storm. God gives the right knowledge and understanding.

Initiative

Having initiative involves starting and sustaining a task or project over time. Initiative is a tricky thing to grasp, especially if one has not been cultured into the practice. There are people who, moved by their passion for some tasks, will not rest till they find a way of achieving their means. Be it a business venture, a burden to help out, a launching of some organization. Others will not move an inch till trouble forces them to creativity; otherwise, in times of peace, they will gladly sit and enjoy the good of the land. And when times of crises come, such a person will buzz with ideas in an unperfected fashion. To others still, this whole matter is a wholly foreign concept. Life is limited to the carefully trodden paths to success, never daring to dream bigger. While the traditional culture may be useful and a worthwhile venture, in some cases, it may have reached the peak of growth. And thus, require a new direction, fresh innovation. Lack of it and the slow death of the enterprise will begin.

Sometimes the youth sit and wait for things to fall into place, something that never happens. Today success requires a lot of input. The world is more competitive than ever before and unforgiving towards mistakes. The youth need to operate with wisdom and divine insight instead of competition or selfish gain. They have to grasp the courage for venturing out, facing the risks, and still succeed. Have the courage to overcome the intimidation from established players in the various fields of life. Courage to make it in a world that is indifferent towards them.

Success in any venture requires continual learning and adjustment. The dynamics in the spheres of life keep on changing constantly, and while we are not to be changing in tandem with shifts in sophisticated styles, we should be adapting to current needs in Godly ways. We have to be classics, remaining relevant in every season with the timeless righteous ways of God. Worthy initiatives arise from people who understand the times, the actions necessary, and how to do it.

Righteousness

Righteousness is often a superficially understood reality by a significant portion of Christian youth. It is a gift from God to all born again Christians. It is a divine pattern, a template for how man is to function on earth. Being declared righteous is God crediting to the believer in Christ an undeserved position, being reconciled to God in Christ, thus becoming a partaker of the divine nature. A righteous person has understood that they overcome sin because they have an incorruptible nature. The Holy Spirit imparts righteousness in the spirit of a believer. The reality of which is evident in the soul and body- in daily living.

We find a big disconnect in those whose minds are unrenewed in the knowledge of righteousness. Who use grace as an excuse to not conform their souls' desires to the reality in their human spirits. The result is a rapid decline in spiritual truths: righteous but free to lie every moment, coarse joking, softening the perversity of sin, corrupted thinking patterns hidden beneath beautiful clothes and deceptive smiles, and stubborn hearts that heed no authority.

Virtues such as love, courage, patience, kindness, honesty are losing appeal. What the media is propagating, promiscuity, individualism, lying, orgies, licentiousness, violence has quickly become the way of life for people. Heroes are no longer the righteous persons; heroes are the lead actors in movies, T.V celebrities, and musicians watering down the gospel. Anything that is prevailing against the specific course of justice is more likely to get attention and a big following. If you question the moral order, you are told not to judge, but evidently, something is very wrong. The decline in the moral compass is an indicator of deep problems in the hearts of people.

The more significant cause for alarm is how fast such corruption is creeping into the church. The devil's attack on God's people often involves a doctrine of the mixture, inserting some impurity into a pure substance. This mixture was the doctrine of Balaam, getting God's people into idolatry and sexual immorality, thus compromising their stand with God. The enemy knows he may not directly shake believers from holding to God, but by compromising them, he wins.

The young generations are facing increased levels of profanity and wickedness. Yet to them are also displayed more magnificent patterns of righteousness. As we study the Bible, we can be a more fabulous example to them. Bearing in mind that God is not slow to justice, whoever chooses to disobey God will, without doubt, reap judgment. The Word says, *"Don't be misled-you cannot mock the justice of God. You will always harvest what you plant." Galatians 6:7*

The Word of God must remain the guide in daily living. Even the most successful people who do not acknowledge God use Biblical principles, every organization today requires employees to conduct themselves in integrity and have a sense of responsibility. Some employers will not allow any of their staff to misbehave out of the workplace; it influences their corporate image. There is no room for faulty behavior in the sphere of excellence. Therefore, live righteously, manifest the spiritual realities given to you by God without covering them with arguments of modernity.

Obsession with Money, Consumerism and Showing Off

Some of the most marketable products are 'how to get rich quick materials.' Videos, books, talk shows that give secrets of getting rich are hot stuff. Consumerism, the preoccupation of society with the acquisition of consumer goods, is a worldwide trend. Consumerism is a way of sustaining business profits and government taxes. Consumerists tend to show off their purchases. Showoff reveals a sense of insecurity about riches, that unless the riches are displayed, there is no satisfaction. If all you feel is an urge to have great wealth, 'so what after that?'

It is more fulfilling to live a meaningful life of adding value to others, offering solutions rather than bleeding the society to achieve personal goals. Generating solutions create wealth as a byproduct of fulfilling work. What we give to people will long be remembered than what we procure for ourselves. When we give ourselves to improve livelihoods, solve problems, our legacies will live long. We will not need to search for fame; it will follow and cling to us.

To avoid the snares, we need to clothe ourselves with an attitude of humility. We must bear in mind that all wealth belongs to God, and we are only His stewards. We are entrusted with wealth to serve His purpose, for our upkeep and to support other people in love. At birth, we come with nothing, and at death, we leave all material possessions on earth. We cannot add any tangible thing to this world except what is already there. Since the earth and all that is in it belongs to God, the thought of amassing material riches for personal gain is not only flawed; it is stealing from God.

The joy of life is living in contentment. *"Godliness with contentment is itself great wealth." (1 Timothy 6:6)*

HINDRANCE TO GROWTH

Sin

Sin, in all its forms, is the chief hindrance to growth. Sin is missing conformity to the image of God, having a nature contrary to the divine nature. Out of this nature springs all manner of disobedience and rebellion against God. A born-again Christian can commit acts of sin arising from an unrenewed mindset.

A person's disobedience to God causes suffering not only for him but also for other people around and far from him. Today many people are suffering not because of their actions but because of the wrongs committed by other people. Individual acts of sin also hinder people from growing in excellence by severely impairing spiritual vision and opening the door for the enemy to launch attacks.

The Lord Jesus paid the penalty for sin. In Him, we are saved from the power of sin and live righteously by His grace. The blood of Jesus destroys all bondages of sin and all curses. The work of the cross is complete, and we can always declare that to the enemy if he dares encroach into our lives.

If we hope to have victory, we ought to live in Christ. Then whether there is sin or righteousness around us, we will be the light and the salt, changing situations for good, overcoming darkness with light, not ones to give in or give up.

Let us consider a few issues in the context of sin:

Corruption

Corruption has hindered many chances of fair employment resulting in feelings of lethargy among the youth. Hopelessness in that any effort put will be in vain. Such desperation is from the enemy keen to snuff out the light in one's life. Many youths get into bribing their way to jobs, forgetting that God hates bribery.

In Kenyan roads currently, travelers sit silent as corrupt traffic officers collect bribes from public transport operators just to avoid delays in travel or being arrested for challenging the officers. In most public and private institutions corruption prevails as an accepted evil against which citizens feel powerless. Sadly, lives are always at stake in a case of corruption; that is why it is so evil. A compromise is never an act of wisdom. People must always make the right decisions concerning human lives. *"Trust in the Lord and do good. Then you will live safely in the land and prosper." Psalms 37:3*

Ethnicity and Racism

We may define ethnicity as belonging to a social group that has a common cultural tradition and language. All human beings have different ethnic origins. There are close to 17,000 people groups or tribes in the World. Ethnic groups represent the diversity of God demonstrated in man. Different people groups break the monotony of a similar culture that would otherwise be from the Arctic to the Antarctic. Diversity enhances living in different environments.

Diversity works well if we let it be, having the capacity to let other people be different as long as whatever they do is not contrary to God's standards. However, we have trouble doing that because we often view our groups as better and wiser than others, as if more privileged or deserving better than the rest. I have seen that education is not enough to bring freedom. After school, all we have are educated ethnocentric with better means of perpetuating hatred and capable of smartly hiding their loathing.

The problems of negative ethnicity and racism are based on faulty social thinking and have no real biological foundation. So why do they persist even when we know the truth that no real differences exist? They are spiritual problems, which cannot be sorted out by academic knowledge. They require spiritual solutions that involve dethroning the demonic principalities promoting hatred.

In Christ, whichever local group or race you come from is of no consequence. All believers belong to the family of God. A divine family out of this World that is sufficient for us. We must also remember that we are work in progress. For some, Christ is well-formed in them. For others, tribal and racial affiliations are still breaking down. So, we should be patient with each other, knowing tomorrow we will be better.

If you succeed, you do not give credit to your tribe or race. You give glory to God. If you fail, you do not blame your tribe, race, or another group. Instead, you look up to God. In the face of negative ethnicity and racism, we are to respond with truth in love. The mind of Christ is free from petty thinking and tribal grouping. Let us not shame the name of our Lord; instead, let us prove to the World that Christ has indeed transformed our lives.

Confusion

The confusion of the World is a big problem for a young mind. And one wonders 'what works and what doesn't?' Peer pressure, societal pressure, and the showbiz of consumerists. Individualism without concern for others, the weight of daily needs, and work. The hypocrisy of men coated in sweetness, the wicked succeeding in their endeavors, and new world order schemes. Mixed priorities and existentialism campaigns: All these forces purport to be true.

In today's World, relative truth has swept off the long-established societal order. One way to identify such a society is where you find people holding tightly to a few ethical principles in a wild storm of confusion. The few morals are often the remains of a once progressive, morally upright society. In some places today, a lie can cost a person his or her job. But no one will bother with the same person if he or she promotes sexual pervasions. While no sin is less evil, the consequences differ.

The Pharisees and the teachers of the law in Israel were careful to tithe even the least income from their herb gardens but did not care about the weightier matters of doctrine- justice, mercy, and faith. As a result of the failures, Israel was scattered and harassed like sheep without a shepherd. And like a drowning man, the leaders opted to clutch at a straw: small things which could not save their lives. While they had the Word of God, darkness swept in because they did not follow the whole counsel. So, it is with today's society that is declining rapidly. Confusion is at its peak when personal desires precede moral values. Today you can expect any news on the screens because many minds are confused.

There is confusion in the church concerning the understanding of Scriptures, permissible behaviors, freedom of believers, and traditions to follow. Dr. G. Campbell's says, "the whole Truth does not lie in 'it is written,' but in 'it is written' and 'again it is written.'" Interpreting the Scriptures is done in light of the whole counsel of God. Remember when the devil was tempting Jesus to jump off from the temple pinnacle quoting the Scriptures? Jesus replied, *"It is also written..." (Matthew 4:5-7).*

'The proud seems to prosper,' the Psalmist notes. Living painless flashy lives, they crush others mercilessly and speak proudly of their wicked schemes. *'What does God know?'* they ask. And the just person wonders *'did I keep myself pure for nothing?'* Till like the Psalmist, one enters the temple of the Lord and then understands the destiny of the wicked. The wicked are on a slippery path that leads to destruction; in a moment, they are no more. The righteous dwell in the shelter of the Most High God who leads them to a glorious destiny. His love endures forever, and His peace He gives to His dear ones, even a sober mind in the face of confusion. (Psalms 73)

THE CASE OF THE ECONOMY

There are bold efforts towards achieving economic growth and realization of political democracy on several fronts in Africa, but that alone cannot solve Africa's problems. Political freedom is good, but along with it often comes secularism that eats away at the moral fabrics of the people. Secularism has been a vital tool of the devil in watering down Christianity. Economic growth does not make living cheaper because taxes increase to cater for the pricey development and maintenance of infrastructure and other facilities. Moreover, world catastrophes can wipe out financial wealth in a moment. So, there is no confidence in economic growth or democracy.

However, a growing economy presents avenues of spurring greater excellence when utilized well. It brings better technologies and more organized life systems that we can leverage to build excellence in our lives. The good news to a believer is that a country's economy does not limit him. God's sons have a higher, more productive kingdom above any national GDP! We are like an ambassador of a country in a foreign nation. Though the ambassador lives in the host nation, he gains support from a different economy. The troubles of the host nation's economy do not hinder him from growth! And that is what we are, ambassadors for Christ on earth!

God's sons prosper anywhere in the World irrespective of the state of the prevailing economic conditions and their success causes economies to grow. Isaac prospered during a famine in Canaan. He harvested a hundredfold of his seed in a dry land where other people were starving. Isaac was not wiser than all the people in Canaan. The secret to his prosperity was his covenant with God. As God's voice guided him, he sowed his seed with diligence and harvested a full measure.

We need God's voice to know when and where to invest our God-given treasures. The harvest is not in some land of fortune; the produce comes from God, the God who blesses. You can prosper in the desert; in the farthest parts of this World, you can prosper greatly.

Way Forward

The ultimate deal is in the individual's standing with God. Unless the Lord prospers a man, his effort will bear nothing. A person must be well equipped with the right knowledge, wisdom, and understanding that will ensure success in this World. A well-equipped man of God can bless millions, even billions of people, but a wicked person cannot. When wealth rests in the hands of the Godly, there is rejoicing and blessing upon the land.

God has given us the capacity for productivity and progress in our living. He has given us vast deposits: resources, different abilities, time, and spiritual gifts. It is like capital for starting a business that He requires us to invest wisely to fulfill His purpose in our lives. But if you eat your deposits, what shall come upon thee?

Every believer must identify the deposit in them and then set out to develop it. All increase is from the deposit, and you cannot bear good fruit if you are not rooted in Christ.

MENTORSHIP

"Plans go wrong for lack of advice; many advisers bring success."
Proverbs 15:22

Mentorship is the art of imparting skills and wisdom to a person done by an elder or an expert. Good mentorship is necessary to save youths with lots of energy but less wisdom. Today, more than ever before, men and women of faith need to arise and shape the lives of youth. Not many people have a clue about what is necessary. Tough economic times force parents to spent most of their time away from the children when they are growing up. The parent-child bond is broken at an early age and never grows again. When the child grows up, it becomes harder for the parent and the child to understand each other, and their perceptions of life are wide apart.

Parenting is no easy task, but here is one key thing: take care of your walk. Live a righteous life. It is who you are that is going to affect your children more than what you say. And even if the children forsake the way of the Lord, they will always have a good example to remind them of the truth. The excellent example needs compliments of great mentors, people who can bring new experience and wealth of knowledge apart from the home experience. But who is worthy of that task?

King Solomon offers a great example in the book of Proverbs. Several times he says, *'my son, listen when your father corrects you, pay attention and learn good judgment' Proverbs 4:1*. Solomon illustrates how wisdom is supreme and beneficial. The precious understanding of the elders is what we need. We need people who can rightly guide young people.

A person's future depends on the decisions made while young. Youth is not a time to enjoy irresponsibly waiting to begin life later. Decisions made follow one through life, giving back fruits of the kind in each stage. So, you would better make choices that add value to life and contribute to your destiny. At youth, you are on the morning of your life, and you need to decide how your day of living is going to be.

To achieve greatness, plan to learn at the feet of a mentor. And especially in venturing into a new field apart from what is normal in your circles. Gamaliel taught Apostle Paul the law, and Paul mentored Timothy. The Lord Jesus prepared the twelve disciples for three years and all of them prospered greatly in their work afterward. At any stage in life, we have to submit ourselves to some higher authority in our environment. Then we tap from the wisdom and administration, and in the case of a ministry, special grace from the spiritual leader.

Choosing a mentor is a delicate affair because if you make a mistake you may end up in the wrong path. You have to examine your potential mentors. It is vital to consider the substance of a person you listen to; you only look to a person who hears from God. Then your life will not be ruined while it buds with promise. A mentor is not final in life since, as an individual, you always have to make the last decision concerning your life. Most crucial, Jesus Christ has the final say. Even the best willing of men may limit you if their vision is far below God's plan.

Be mentored rightly, and then at your time, you will mentor others well. The wisdom of living currently is with the generation of yesterday. And the understanding of living for the coming age will be found in the current generation. There is always passing the baton. And the baton is not a bag of responsibilities; it is the wisdom of the elders. It is the deep insight from God, given to the younger by the elder.

We, as individuals, a church, community, society, country, have to develop comprehensive mentorship programs for our people. It is not just the youth who need mentorship. All members of society do need it. Then we will build a healthy community that has accountability and a sense of direction.

THE STRENGTH OF THE YOUTH

The young have a lot as their advantage in improving their lives. Every good thing comes from the Lord, and the one who commits their life to God will live a victorious life. God is the source of all life, and He gives all we need for living, be it wisdom, strength, or protection.

"He gives power to the weak and strength to the powerless. Even youths will become weak and tired, and young men will fail in exhaustion. But those who trust in the Lord will find new strength. They will soar high on wings like eagles. They will run and not grow weary. They will walk and not faint." Isaiah 40: 29-31.

The youth indeed have the strength to carry out several activities, the energy to pursue goals relentlessly. Strength is a vital thing for any endeavor. However, human power quickly fails under the strain of work and only God can renew it. Most of the big international corporations currently were formed by people in their early years. The young developers built the corporations throughout their lives. Initiatives started at a tender age stand a bigger chance of expansive growth.

Young people are often flexible and adaptive to changes in a better way than older folk. That means they can work in almost any habitable area of the World and still find joy in their work. They can change careers and adapt quickly. The young people do not have many burdens attached to their lives, which allows them to focus their efforts more productively and forge productive cooperation. The young at heart do not bear deep-rooted biases; they are open to expansion, interaction with people from all walks of life, and openness to change.

Being young means, you have a lot of people to learn from, the younger, the age mates, and the older people ahead. There is lots of experience to learn from without having to live through it. It is more comfortable at that period to elevate attitudes and beliefs from humanistic to Godly ones. As it is said, shaping a piece of wood happens when it is green, not when dry.

The young are quick learning; they seem to grasp concepts fast. This fastness is so handy when it comes to a fast-changing world, fast-paced operating systems that require quick decision making with no room for error. Thinking and acting fast requires a dynamic mind that can analyze a situation in short moments and render a sound judgment. God's seasons are shifting more quickly, requiring hearts and minds that can let go of the old and embrace the new. The young have the chance to lead God's revival moves on the earth.

The young believer has won the battle with the evil one. He has overcome the vanity of the World and sees life in the big view of eternity. He is privileged to make plans and investments that count for all of the eternity future. From the cross of Calvary, the young have found victory in the Lord. On account of the win, all they have to do is live fulfilling lives by standing. This standing is one of a good conscience and faith.

The youth find the power to pursue their dreams. They have the time to mold ideas. While the old at heart reminisce of the good old times, the young at heart rejoice in the present and the future. The ones who have newness of life rejoice over things they will never get to experience personally. King David never got to see the temple Solomon built, but he was happy that his son would make it.

PRAYER

'Prayer is the timeless discipline for all who believe in God'

Prayer attracts much interest in the Christian circles, but less practice in daily living. We all know how vital it is in our lives, but it has not been more natural to pray. You have seen a passionate prayer group collapse after some time, or your prayers grinding to a halt with all manner of excuses.

Prayer is the saint's communion that connects him with God. Through it, the believer fellowships with God as he passes from the earth praises, thanksgiving, petition, and requests in holy adoration of the Almighty. Faithful praying comes from the Holy Spirit's activity in our spirits and moves into His supernatural realm. The Spirit of God guides effective praying. The Holy Spirit searches the mind of God and reveals to us what is God's will.

Every activity of the believer ought to be initiated and activated in prayer. It is the prerequisite of undertaking what matters before God. How else will you proceed to serve God without knowing what He desires of you, or how can you presume to know what to do without the Lord's guidance? Prayer is essential, and we should pray as often as Jesus did. ***"Jesus often withdrew to the wilderness for prayer." Luke 5:16***. Prayer has to be made consistently in great depth.

Fewer Christians have reached the intensity of prayer witnessed in the life of our Lord Jesus. He often spent full nights in prayer alone. Today we usually need good numbers and music to make it to the morning. Night prayers filled with activity not related to communing with God. Noise has little to do with effective prayer. An unhurried communion with the Father often demands moments of solitude away from distractions of daily life. Like our Lord, our prayer volume ought to be full days.

Effective prayer requires a close relationship with God, beginning with salvation and then a close walk with Him, led by the Holy Spirit.

When a believer is close to God, he understands the mind of God and prays accurately. The Lord finds pleasure in answering the prayer of His close friend. It is to such a person that God answers before the prayer made. But if you are far from God, your requests will often be self-centered, lacking the illumination of the Holy Spirit. A close relationship with God grows in constant fellowship with Him. The Lord loves those who seek his face, and He never hides from them.

Again, and again, God has promised us, *"Keep on asking, and you will receive what you ask for. Keep on seeking, and you will find. Keep on knocking, and the door will be opened to you. For everyone who asks, receives. Everyone who seeks, finds. And to everyone who knocks, the door will be opened." Matthew 7:7.* We cannot receive what we ask in a wrong manner, because God is just in His ways! At times I have made prayers, which I later regretted and repented for, seemingly honest and honorable requests only realizing then how selfish I was.

Prayer is not the point of pouring everything to God then fleeing immediately. It is a time of communicating with God, listening to Him as He speaks. In His presence, the heart receives sanctification. The believer can, therefore, pour their heart honestly.

The fundamental way of communing with God is by praying His Word. Studying the Word in prayer as the Holy Spirit imparts in your heart revelation of the Word. I have found this method advantageous because the will of God is in His Word, and the Word is the language of prayer. So, the moment you are praying through the Word as revealed, you grasp the Rhema word for the season. You understand what the Lord is doing and what you would rather be doing at the time.

In prayer, we find victory, the forgiveness of sins, restoration, the revelation of mysteries, breakthrough, renewal of strength, we receive life as we interact with our God. In prayer, we experience heaven while on earth. Through prayer, the devil's schemes fail, and captives are free. Gifts are activated, and ministries birthed. Daniel was a man gifted with the ability to interpret the meanings of visions and dreams, whose implications he understood in prayer.

Today many gifts and talents are wasting away because of prayerlessness. Great ministries are lost when complacent believers get contented with mediocre living. Any great victory must be won and sustained by prayer. Any man who desires excellence must be soaked in prayer and must pray with understanding to know an answered prayer.

Prayer must be honest, not fabricated, speaking truthful words, exact circumstances, and declaring the spiritual realities in non-conforming environments. Paul says in **Romans 12: 3, "...do not think you are better than you really are. Be honest in your evaluation of yourselves, measuring yourselves by the faith God has given us."**

The prayer of Jesus in John chapter 17 illustrates the clarity, honesty, and fervency of effective prayer. It is a genuine prayer made before the Father in the simplest of terms, not with useless babbling or mere repetition. One of the critical lessons we get from it is the focus of prayer. Prayer centers on God. The Lord Jesus's prayer is a model for us to follow; in our prayers, we must be inclined to what glorifies God and accomplishes His purpose. We exist for His purpose, and apart from Him, our lives have no meaning.

We should ignore the temptations of trying to impress God with lofty words. He is the source of all understanding and knowledge, and our efforts to please Him with words fall short of worthiness. Appealing words are not detestable before Him, on the contrary, in our adoration, the minds light up with words of great affection, and the heart with emotions and groans. Our languages are insufficient in revealing the spiritual.

We ought to remain prayerful and keep growing in the practice of prayer. A crucial indicator of growth in prayer is the composition. If you keep on praying over the same issues, it could as well mean you are only concerned with your life and maybe a few people around you. A growing prayer life will have an increasing scope of depth, coverage, and focus, expanding from the local area and self to selfless worship of God and burden over other believers all over the World.

As mentioned earlier, we are moved to prayer by the Holy Spirit. Thus, it is borne out of deep conviction. Prayer cannot be dry and dull when led by the Spirit. However, there are moments of dryness, and a believer should persist until there is a breakthrough. Prayer is warfare; therefore, we must remember the devil will try his best to hinder us from praying. Persist in prayer, day and night soak your life in prayer. Commit your plans to God, surrender your desires and dreams to Him to fulfill. We gain means for life in prayer.

From Scripture examples, we understand that God answers prayer the moment we make it or even before we pray. The manifestation of the answer depends on the duration necessary to form a spiritual reality in the physical, the knowledge, and understanding needed to receive.

It is important to note that not every moment is for prayer and that everything is not sorted out in prayer. After praying and receiving God's instruction, action must be made and not hide from duty. We have a part to play as God accomplishes His work. He partners with us in His work, we should never think it is all upon God to complete everything as we sit idly unless the Lord guides us otherwise.

Prayer is not independent of other worthy practices, and in the next chapter, we will look at other vital complementary elements that are birthed by prayer.

VITAL ELEMENTS IN CULTIVATING EXCELLENCE

There are some things so vital in cultivating excellence that without them, we cannot hope to get anywhere. They are like building blocks for a building, without which it cannot rise. If I would omit them then this book Would be incomplete. So, let us have a look.

Faith

Faith is a firm, unshakable belief in something or someone. According to Hebrews 11, *faith is the substance of things hoped for*, so it is the basis for what we hope. The manner of faith determines our expectations. Biblical faith is faith towards God.

"And it is impossible to please God without faith. Anyone who wants to come to Him must believe that God exists and that He rewards those who sincerely seek Him." Hebrews 11:6

To us, faith is believing that God is who He says He is, that is our Father. And that He rewards us when we seek Him; that is, we become like Him. The evidence that we have found God is we become like Him. Our God is the perfection of excellence. We become excellent by getting conformed to the nature and likeness of God. Our sure belief is that the Father will continually impart excellence in us.

The challenge to faith is doubt. It is easy to trust God for a short time, but if help tarries, faith crumbles, and the man helps himself out. Even brief moments of trouble can be detrimental. Doubts begin, unbelief takes root, no longer sure whether God is interested.

The Israelites on their journey from Egypt manifested doubt and unbelief like we often do. They wondered, 'the Lord parted the red sea... but is He able to feed us?' 'He fed us... but is He able to quench our thirst?' 'He provided water... but can He do it again? On a day they were to enter Canaan (and Canaan to us is a place of spiritual fullness - Zion), belief shipwrecked their destiny and inheritance. We have them as an example in regards to disbelief. We have a better Canaan in Christ, a place of spiritual fullness, a place of excellence, a place of rest. Have you entered into your rest? Or are you mark timing on the road to the fullness thereof? Faith is mandatory to enter God's rest.

Without the continuous exercise of faith, lukewarm attitudes and personal assumptions quickly replace the firmness of conviction. Time becomes the expected key of transformation, yet time does not change a thing either improve anyone. Time has no more application in our endeavors than the effort we put. The timing of things in our dispensation is dependent upon us receiving divine knowledge into a particular matter. Accessing knowledge fulfills the timing of issues. What we call God's timing is a moment that is dependent on us receiving knowledge according to His revelation. Without this understanding, life can be full of desperation by the passing of days.

To sustain active faith, we must always see life in the light of eternity. The eternal perspective means having insight beyond time, having the big picture of how God works, and the functioning of His kingdom. *Ephesians 1:11 says, "...He makes everything work out according to His plan."* His plan or will is to conform us to His image, Christ. Whatever we hope for in our lives must be viewed in the lens of becoming like Christ.

Conforming to Christ is an all-dimension endeavor, not just moral perfection. It includes but not limited to divine health, prosperity, and access to grace at the revelation of Jesus Christ. In this regard, God is giving all that we need for life and godliness, being more willing than we are to see the perfection of our lives. Therefore, we trust God and have peace.

The emphasis on having faith is that among the spiritual gifts of the Holy Spirit is the gift of faith. This gift of faith enables a believer to trust God for mighty workings in a particular situation. To serve God, we need faith. It is impossible to please God without faith.

We cultivate faith through hearing the Word of God, the living Word, which activates our trust in God and causes Him to move powerfully in our lives. Hearing the Word is listening to a sent one sharing the Word. By faith we attain victory over challenges or victory in the problems like the writer of the book of Hebrews notes in chapter 11: 32-38. How some heroes of faith *"...overthrew kingdoms, ruled with justice, and received what God had promised them. They shut the mouths of lions, quenched the flames of fire, and escaped death by*

the edge of the sword. Their weakness was turned to strength." Others
*"...were tortured, jeered at, and their backs were cut open with whips,
chained in prisons, some were stoned, sawn in half, killed by the sword."*

All the categories obtained a victory by faith. Though some
conquered their situations physically, others seemingly destroyed still got
a win. Today the triumph of faith is still two ways. Whichever way you
go through, be victorious. The victory of faith is to become conformed
to Christ in any situation you go through.

The Will of God

"Furthermore, because we are united with Christ, we have received an inheritance from God, for He chose us in advance, and He makes everything work out according to His plan." Ephesians 1:11

God's will is what He wants to do on earth, either in a person's life, family, a group, church, a nation, or nations. It is His purpose for a person or persons at a particular time. God's will is that we become His exact representatives on earth.

We have the responsibility of continually seeking what God wants to do and the way we are to follow. Seeking God's will means pursuing a lifestyle that best represents God. It means entrusting your decisions to the One who cannot fail you. The will of God is the best for us. We have a free will in us by which we make choices. A free-will means we have freedom of choice. Seeking God's will means surrendering our will to His, aligning our will with His. It is submitting our freedom of choice to His guidance. Submitting to the will of God is a daily endeavor for the believer.

"The Spirit searches the mind of God and shows us his deep secrets. No one can know a person's thoughts except that person's spirit, and no one can know God's thoughts except God's own Spirit. And we have received God's Spirit (not the world's spirit), so we can know the wonderful things God has freely given us." 1 Corinthians 2:10-12

God has provided the means to know His will for our lives. When His Spirit is in us, His thoughts become our thoughts and His ways our ways. To sustain such a union of purpose with God, we have to hear correctly as the Holy Spirit speaks to our hearts and obey Him. God's desire is suitable for all who trust in Him. The Bible is full of promises for the faithful, which we can never exhaust in our lifetime.

The will of God from the beginning has been to conform us to Christ. Thus, whatever God does on earth is in line with bringing us to the perfection of Christ — making us like Him. When we devote time to study the Bible, the Holy Spirit reveals to us the mind of the Father concerning our lives. If you do not know what to do or say, spend your time prayerfully studying the Bible. He also ministers to us through dreams, visions, instant thoughts, and even during prayer. He speaks to our conscience by His Spirit, He speaks to us through other people, and He speaks to us in many more ways. The key is learning to discern His voice from other voices.

We can become short-sighted in the rat race and miss the point. We can lose the right understanding of God's unlimited power under the weight of suffering. However, God is well able, we should not compare Him to money, wealth or any created thing. God has put desires in our hearts for various fields in life. In seeking Him, we often find that what is in us is His desire. So, we surrender all the more to have such a passion perfected and worked out by him.

What should you do if in seeking compliance with Christ, you do not discern the path? If in desiring to hear Him speak to your heart, you hear nothing? There is no doubt that God hears our cries each day and that He answers our requests. We need not be worried in such cases, and just need to wait upon Him patiently. Let your heart be attentive to His instruction, and it shall be well with you.

We can eliminate false voices from our lives by using the filter of God's Word. Heeding only to the one voice that leads us to the speaking, actions, directions, environments, activities that best help form Christ in us and other peoples' lives. For example, the question of whether it is God's will to work in a particular organization can be answered by first understanding that work is God's idea. We work primarily to represent God before considering the remuneration. So, is working in a particular organization a platform for serving God? If yes, then you can go on to find what is your assignment for the season, the remuneration and any other factor you may have. You will realize that God will guide your life accurately.

Passion

Passion is the deeply stirring emotion that is unstoppable towards some activity. It is also an unwavering affection for someone. Passion is the heart of real action and is often cultivated in a person over time, mostly divine in origin, not a thing you grab in a day and run with it. Passion defies half-heartedness at work and employs the best of efforts and energy in a person to pursue a goal.

"I don't mean to say that I have already achieved these things or that I have already reached perfection. But I press on to possess that perfection for which Christ first possessed me. No, my dear brothers and sisters, I have not achieved it, but I focus on one thing: forgetting the past and looking forward to what lies ahead, I press on to reach the end of the race and receive the heavenly prize for which God, through Christ Jesus, is calling us." (Philippians 3:12-14)

Great passion is in the heart of a man who has caught a vision, an illumination of the beauty of God's plans. Christ, who is the mystery and master plan of God, perfects our visions. In Christ, the truth never loses meaning as Paul says, *"I will rejoice even if I lose my life, pouring it out like a liquid offering to God..." Philippians 2: 17.*

The Lord Jesus Christ loves you, and you can be a choice vessel for Him. He can stir passion in you for exceptional work in His kingdom. You, too, like Paul, can set out with zeal unstoppable by human frailties for God's universal plan. So today, begin cultivating a passion for whatever God is calling you to, He will give the grace to sustain it.

Passion is infectious and moves with speed. A passionless life is a cold one, the kind that cannot influence for good. A passionless life is detestable before God, who wrought your salvation in grand passion. You need passion to move. You need it more to influence people in a particular direction. And it is not something hidden; it is visible, tangible, and knows no limit in price.

What do you have? The Lord will use it. You need to get a vision of the end, gather your light, and go light the world. God needs you to impact the world with His view. You must not travel all over to do this. From your room, you can do it, in prayer, and then set out to do what Christ has gotten hold of you.

Fear of the Lord

The fear of God is a great thing to have. To fear God is to hate evil and revere God in selfless worship. It is only the man who has seen God who knows what it is to fear the Lord. Since no one can see God and live, those who have seen have died and risen anew.

"It is all over! I am doomed, for I am a sinful man. I have filthy lips, yet I have seen the King" Isaiah 6:5. Isaiah cried when he saw God exalted in glory. Before the Lord, Isaiah lay bare his iniquity all clear. Isaiah learned how to fear God.

The presence of God brings sin to light. Nothing can stand the glorious presence of the Almighty. Isaiah changed by the encounter with the Lord, cries, *"...here I am. Send me." Isaiah 6:8.* He would never be the same again. So is Ezekiel when he saw the glory of the Lord, glorious yet terrifying. The kind of terror that is divine in origin and which brings reverence for God.

Before the Lord, the believer feels overwhelmed and insufficient, yet there is nowhere else to go, there is the life found. He cannot help but respond in worshipping the God who has conquered his soul. And so sweet is the worship of a broken man before his Maker.

It is the people who have seen the Lord who know what it means to fear the Lord. Every human pretense, excuses, and the snares that often trip man flee away. The fear of the Lord is not fear of punishment since the man who experiences it is righteous. It is something more profound, the feeling of been undone before a holy God. The fear brings knowledge and understanding to the piety believer, and he begins to see things in light of God. Such a man will excel. He is the one who has seen God and lived. Such a man has in his heart the disposition for purity and holiness.

We need the illumination of the Holy Spirit if we are to know God worthily. It is not possible to worship God; you do not know. People can build an altar for an unknown God, but their sacrifices become polluted.

How can a man offer himself as a holy sacrifice to a God whose rules he does not fathom?

God reveals Himself to us in many ways; through His Word, creation, visions, and dreams. By His Spirit, He convicts us concerning His divine nature. We cannot help but fall to our knees in holy reverence of God. We cannot help but willingly and in brokenness fear the Lord, worship the Lord of all creation.

Motive

A motive is a reason behind someone's actions, the driving force of activity. Each of our actions and words derives impetus from a motive in our hearts, whether consciously or unconsciously. An act can only be noble or base as the motive behind it.

"The human heart is the most deceptive of all things, and desperately wicked. Who knows how bad it is, but I, the Lord, searches all hearts and examines secret motives. I give all people their due rewards, according to what their actions deserve." (Jeremiah 17:9-10)

"If I could speak all the languages of earth and angels, but did not love others, I would only be a noisy gong or a clanging cymbal. If I had the gift of prophecy, and if I understood all of God's secret plans and possessed the knowledge, and if I had such faith that I could move mountains, but did not love others, I would be nothing. If I gave everything I have to the poor and even sacrificed my body, I could boast about it, but if I did not love others, I would have gained nothing." 1 Corinthians 13:1-3.

Nothing matters without love, be it faith, prophecy, or giving. They all fade out in the absence of love. The way to judge motive is whether it arises from love. Anything else but love drags all initiatives down the drain. And any action furthered without love cannot be appealing before God. We must examine and let the Lord search our hearts daily. Because God is love, anything without love is without God and will not count before the Father.

It is effortless to forget the weight of motives in the busy schedules of daily life. Brethren have fallen to this trap, heaping burdens over themselves in service. What a shock will be there before the judgment seat of Christ, when a man expecting a crown will only survive as one rescued from a fire, and a lifetime of activity only comparable to straw.

How many times have people, condemned by their conscience and desiring to appease it; have cunningly engaged in giving. A giving not of love but a selfish motive of building a name. How many activities are for showing off power and influence rather than love for people.

"Love is patient and kind. Love is not jealous or boastful or rude. It does not demand its way. It is not irritable, and it keeps no record of being wronged. It does not rejoice about injustice but rejoices whenever the truth wins out. Love never gives up, never loses faith, is always hopeful, and endures through every circumstance." 1 Corinthians 13:4-7.

Love is not emotional; it is not a feeling. Love is a principle of commitment that requires laying down one's life for the person you love. Loving means committing to a course of action that consistently benefits others. There is no excellence without love. Love is the more excellent way.

Wisdom

Wisdom is a treasure from God, something we are all welcomed to seek. Wisdom is the divine insight into plans of God that enables one to apply the Truth in a real-life situation. Wisdom calls out to men, *"how long, you simpletons, will you insist on being simpleminded?" Proverbs 1:22*. A simple person knows not how to act wisely; everything he does is of the ordinary type. Simple implies you cannot rise to a superior level of living because you have no clue or interest. That is why the simple insists on living his way away from correction.

"My child listen to what I say and treasure my commands. Tune your ears to wisdom, and concentrate on understanding. Cry out for insight, and ask for understanding. The Lord grants wisdom! From his mouth come knowledge and understanding." Proverbs 2:1-3, 6

Through wisdom, we know what is right, just, and fair. In it, we find the right way to go in safety. True wisdom comes from the Lord, not from men, and with it, He gives understanding. What men give are mere philosophies handed down over generations. What we call wisdom apart from God is often half-truth, and if seen in the light of the Word will be found wanting. The heart that is not illuminated by the Word of God clings to faulty ideas.

People have learned to beautifully craft their lives in patterns of honesty, nobility, and other great virtues. It is trickier than ever to know the genuine person. And often, many have fallen to fraudster tricks losing lots of wealth. If anyone hopes to succeed, there is a great need for wisdom. Without it, you are going down, and you will not know what hit you.

Christ is the wisdom of God. The church manifests God's wisdom to the world and the rulers of darkness. It is wisdom in our actions and prayer that gives us victory over principalities and demons, demonstrating to them the wisdom of God. It is by the wisdom of God that we show our sonship.

"The son of man, on the other hand, feasts and drinks, and you say, 'He's a glutton and a drunkard, and a friend of tax collectors and other sinners!' but wisdom is shown to be right by its results." Matthew 11:19

The impartation of wisdom requires a close relationship with God. It is not a full package you pick in a moment and leave. Seeking God's wisdom involves walking with him, meditating on His Word each day and night, and receiving at the place of prayer. Wisdom is Spirit, a dimension of the Holy Spirit. There is, therefore, no limit to acquiring wisdom.

How I desire that with wisdom, we may also seek spiritual discernment; this type of insight is a gift of the Holy Spirit. A gift of discerning spirits, to know which work is of the Holy Spirit and which is not. Counterfeits, deceptions, and delusions are in every corner of today's living, and you never know what is there till you discern the truth.

The work of false shepherds is to steal, kill, and destroy. Once they take, they happily dangle the exploits before the rightful owners like a carrot in exchange for their lives. The naive man following human wisdom sells his life to get a portion of what was his in the first place. In ignorance, he loses his rights and life.

If you are wise with the wisdom of God, you will not waste your life. You will walk in safety in the paths of the Lord. *"The paths of the Lord are true and right, and righteous people live by walking in them," Hosea 14:9.* You know, the righteous have the right beliefs. If you have the correct beliefs, you will live right.

There was a wise man, so wise was he that King David sought his counsel. Every word this Ahithophel spoke seemed as though it had come directly from the mouth of God. But his story ended sorrowfully and in disgrace because, in his wisdom, he did not seek to honor God and defend justice. He lacked understanding. Understanding is an insight into how things work.

There was a man presented in the book of Acts chapter six, who excelled in wisdom much. He solved the welfare challenges facing the first church. No opposing voice from the Jews could challenge him. Here is a bit of the testimony written about him.

"...they chose the following: Stephen (a man full of faith and the Holy Spirit)" Acts 6:5.

"None of them was able to stand against the wisdom and Spirit by which Stephen spoke." Acts 6:10

Stephen was full of Christ, even to the extent that he saw Christ as He is, exalted in glory. Becoming excellent is becoming Christ-like.

[Job laments that men make great effort to seek material treasures even from the depths of the earth, but they do not discern the value of wisdom neither do they seek it. He goes on the say that wisdom and understanding come from God, that they are not found in the land of the living.]

OTHER KEY ELEMENTS

Motivation

Motivation is the inner drive to do things, to achieve something, to develop, and keep moving forward. Whether it is intrinsic or extrinsic in origin, motivation is vital to a person's endeavors. Intrinsic motivation is the motivation driven by an interest or joy in the task engaged in, and it is internal, not relying on external factors. It is a natural tendency that is critical in personal development. Intrinsic motivation is more or less the same as passion, but while passion is singular in action, motivation maybe on several fronts and smaller scale. Extrinsic motivation has reference to performing an activity to attain an outcome; this may be in part intrinsic if the motivating factor is of high value. The external factors include rewards and competition.

Motivation is the source of the initiative discussed earlier. It is the bit that moves a person to start some activity for a particular cause. We should let ourselves be motivated. It is what makes people move and highlights greatness in a person. Indeed, most of the people who have made significant achievements in life have had strong and unique motivations.

A person without motivation for a worthy cause will settle for less than the best. A motivational drive must be enduring and one that can overcome all hindrances to achieve a goal and not a faint-hearted endeavor. We all can nurture our motivations to a higher level, even build new motivations that were previously unknown to us and also pull-down unworthy ones. Therefore, we have no excuse than to be motivated rightly.

However, motivation alone means little until action is put in place to achieve the desired goal. And if activity and its results are to be a noble cause, the reasoning or the motive behind it must be a worthy one. The motive must be right, and we talked earlier about love being the only ethical motive behind all our actions, whether it is a quest for excellence in some sport, fight for justice, academic achievement, or business growth. Love for God, above all else, love for other people and love for oneself too. Self-love should never degenerate into selfish ambition, where, to succeed, a person causes deserving people to fail.

Here is an example to distinguish between motive and motivation. In a case of reaching out to people in need, a giver's motive maybe love for the people, but the motivation (what stimulates the person continually) is the joy of seeing satisfied people.

Humor

Humor is what amuses people; it is fun. It is an excellent ingredient that spices up life and breaks down stress to open up things clouded with anxiety and worry. Humor brings a light of cheers on the weary face and helps build stronger relationships. Humor can bring a smile on the teary child and inspire hope in the young one.

It is difficult to describe the sound, good humor without confusing it with the versions we find on T.V. screens, the internet, and what people of today love. Good fun should not be at the expense of a person's dignity, comfort, or character. Good humor does not make light of the Word of God, nor does it reference man with diminutive terms. Good fun is the celebration of the Lord's joy released into our lives. It is important to remember what happened to the 42 youths when they made fun of Elisha. They went after him shouting, *"go away, baldy!"* and that was their last laugh before two bears mauled them to death.

We have to get it right, seeing that we have to account for every careless word before God. Today it is common to see comedians on television making fun of preachers and making fun of God too! Stepping into matters they do not understand, dragging with them the naive revelers of the supposed joke.

What seems fun nowadays is no fun at all, fun in blatant iniquity and coarse joking. Humor does not mean compromising standards to earn a light moment. It is common for a person to make a profane joke or lie only to apologize later, 'It was just a joke.' Such is never a joke.

Joy is something not found in the devils' kingdom, not even a trace of it. The devil never has a day of rest, neither his servants. In his place, there is nothing to laugh about, nothing to rejoice. And the devil seeks to spread his bitterness to people on earth. In the kingdom of God, there is endless joy, which is strength and gives health to the bones. There is fun, the celebration of this joy.

There is more humor in dignity, much sweeter humor in respectful engagements. We would be grossly wrong to imagine God does not love humor, to think that we have to go off the mark to earn a laugh. There is super fun in heaven and so on earth.

God has a great sense of fun evident throughout the Scriptures. First, in the kinds of unique creatures, how He laughs at the wicked trying to plot counsel against Him, giving Jacob a wrestling chance, and the Lord Jesus having fun at parties (until He was accused Him of being a glutton and a drunkard.)

Faithfulness

Faithfulness is the unfailing loyalty to someone irrespective of the circumstances or the cost incurred. Faithfulness requires a lot of commitment and the readiness to pay whatever sacrifice is necessary. Throughout the Bible, we find calls upon man to be faithful to God. It is one thing that God requires of us, and for which He will not rest until we turn to him fully.

We express our loyalty to God in various areas; in service, giving, worship, time spent in His presence, resources we give to His work, our bodies. Faithfulness touches on every aspect of our lives concerning God.

"If my people who are called by my name will humble themselves and pray and seek my face and turn from their wicked ways, I will hear from heaven and will forgive their sins and restore their land." (2 Chronicles 7:14)

Throughout history, man has been in constant rebellion to this call, continually getting into grave sins in total defiance of loyalty to God. Humans have shown their preference for the heavy burdens of the enemy over the easy yoke of God.

It is easy to tithe from a KES 10,000 salary faithfully. But once promotion comes, a person may find it unthinkable to give a tithe from a 1-million-shilling salary. It is easy to go for an evangelism mission when young, but when age and affluence begin, unfounded nobility sets in to the detriment of a once passionate evangelist. Man's loyalty to God tends to fade as the cost increases, but the Lord never lets unbearable temptations our way.

"Here is a trustworthy saying, if we die with him, we will also live with him. If we endure hardship, we will reign with him. If we deny him, he will deny us. If we are unfaithful, he remains faithful, for he cannot deny who he is." (2 Timothy 2:11-13)

This kind of faithfulness is a nature built by God in the believer. When the Lord is calling us to faithfulness, He is calling us to be like

Him, to be partakers of His very nature. Loyalty is an eternally enduring attribute.

Today the testimony of Christianity is eroding at a fast rate. Alternative religions are rising powerfully, offering solutions where Christians seem to be slow to act. They are not out to dialogue with us or seek to understand. They want more people in their ranks.

Faithfulness means being a good steward of what we manage. We should hold on till the Lord comes, not to let things go unchecked in the hope of leaving earth when Christ appears. It is the righteous who will ultimately remain on the planet, not the wicked.

WHAT WE MUST DO

'There is something for each of us to do, a noble work for every suitable vessel.'

The key to a meaningful life is living one's purpose. ***"From one man he created all the nations throughout the whole earth. He decided beforehand when they should rise and fall, and he determined their boundaries." Acts 17:26.*** You see, God is specific in detail. Nothing happens by chance. And the things we do are not new to Him, for He knows everything and has ordered our lives according to His divine plan.

We all have a purpose of accomplishing while we live on earth. The purpose covers every aspect of our lives, and all the elements should fit into it. When the purpose is not clear, discontent and time-wasting are inevitable. A proper understanding of purpose unlocks grace for life. The purpose has to do with the talents, the spiritual gifts, the desires, passions, and callings God has put in us.

Natural Talents

Everyone has some talent deposited in them; no one can rightly claim they have none. It is clear that talent and skills are things God has lovingly bestowed upon all men. God's talents in us are to help us live meaningful lives serving Him, supporting ourselves and other people. They're firstly for the glory of God and then personal and common good. No man on earth is without means to fend for self. Indeed, God loves humankind.

Some talents manifest more than others, such that someone may discover his or her talent at an early age while another will take decades to know what is in them. There is such variation in ability than we can exhaust in studying them. Even within the same talent, there is variation. A musician may be more talented than another, yet both are gifted musicians.

Some people seem to know what they are to do at a tender age; others have to explore their lives searching for clues of who they are. A lack of a clear identity often precipitates confusion. Identity crisis is plaguing millions of people in the world today. They cannot figure out who they are, let alone what they can do. The cry is primarily among the youth.

Having an identity means one has an origin. Our origin is God, our creator. He is our Father, and we are His sons. We are not just sons. We are firstborn sons in Christ. *"For God knew his people in advance, and He chose them to become like his Son so that his Son would be the firstborn among many brothers and sisters." Romans, 8:29.* The term 'firstborn' as used means having the priority in all matters. Therefore, we are God's priority before all things.

All we need to do is to seek Him. In seeking, He reveals what He expects of us. He works with us to set out our destiny. The devil in his cunning schemes has formulated several ideas to hide this truth —

theories of evolution and atheism all target identity. Without real identity, people live artificial, fake lives.

Our identity is precious. Each day I live, I bear the mark of a firstborn son and the citizenship of heaven; I dare not accept anything less. You, too, must understand yourself. Then once you know and bear your identity, you will know the Lord's deposit in you.

Sadly, many talents are being wasted in the world. Hearing most secular songs and the instrumentals reveals great talent been used for lesser purposes. The devil has a strategy of stealing the best for his works. Most of the world's renowned secular musicians are hugely gifted, but their talents are going to ruin apart from Christ. Others include top-notch scientists, entertainers, doctors, and leaders using their skills to deny the existence of the God who created and gifted them.

Discovering one's purpose means getting on the right track for life. There is great fulfillment and joy in living out purpose, which is what the Lord has planned for us. We need not live miserable lives doing things we dislike except for the money. Our lives must be spent well on worthy endeavors. *"And just as each person is destined to die once and after that comes judgment," Hebrews 9:27*. To whom shall we be compared to, the servant who went and hid his talent instead of investing it or the other two who earned a hundred percent out of their invested money? (Matthew 25:14-30).

Spiritual Gifts

Another area of interest for every believer is Spiritual gifting. The Holy Spirit gives every believer a gift or gifts. It is important to note that the Holy Spirit distributes the gifts as He desires, and it is not our choice to make. Gifting can be more confusing than the area of talent because talents are natural abilities, which are easily identifiable.

A Spiritual gift is an ability given by the Holy Spirit to each believer, which enables the believer to do a particular work in the church. The Holy Spirit can give multiple gifts to one individual depending on the ministry ordained for the person. Moreover, the Scriptures do encourage believers to desire spiritual gifts. Thus, God can give more gifts to one person based on their desire to serve God.

For our study purpose, we will classify some of them into three categories.

Gifts of speech - prophecy, tongues, interpretation of tongues.

Gifts of revelation - word of knowledge, word of wisdom, discerning of spirits.

Special abilities – faith, working miracles, healings.

There are graces that are often misunderstood as gifts of the Holy Spirit. These include administrations, helps, and the fivefold ministry. The graces are a special appointment given to selected individuals by God as is detailed by Paul in 1 Corinthians 12:28. To every believer is given a specific grace for service. As such, every believer should seek to determine their ministry to the body of Christ. An individual's ministry area is often characterized by a heart burden for particular problems. For example, an administrator is always bothered by inefficiencies and disorganization in the church. Similarly, an evangelist is disproportionately burdened by the sight of unregenerated humanity. Responding to the burden in the heart is a key discovering one's ministry area.

Utilizing Talents in Life

The road to following our passion is not always easy, often it can be tough to get to the field of choice, and a person may end up in a zone least desired. A person who loves banking may lack a job opportunity in a bank and land elsewhere as a hotelier. And since the person needs funds for daily living, it will be more challenging to switch from there. This case is happening to millions of people to a point where the priority in seeking a job is to be somewhere, then the rest will follow.

Getting a job is undoubtedly an excellent relief for any jobless person. It comes as a break from dependency to a level of greater independence and ability to make own decisions freely. Yet the challenge is working only for the money; money being the motivation is less fulfilling. It becomes a trap, and such a person will not settle. The longing will always be for something better. Some people do manage to break from that by seeking more fulfilling careers while others quit altogether, starting the enterprises they love. Like when a person leaves the corporate world to start a school or follow God's calling in full-time church ministry. Still, others learn to adapt their passions to their present jobs or create a specialization where they can serve comfortably in the same organization. An example may be a journalist working in the public relations department of a bank.

Whichever the occupation one gets into, it is vital to adapt oneself to a challenging and fulfilling position or, if possible, shift to where one loves depending on the chances and ability. A life spent at the wrong table will undoubtedly bring a crisis of disappointment and dissatisfaction as time catches up with the person.

The Place of Ministry

Serving God is the primary responsibility in life; it is the lifestyle of the believer. The Christian life is all about God, and He is the foundation and the goal of everything we do. Often service to God is limited to the church setting or going to missions, but that is only a portion of it. Service extends but not limited to our homes, marriage, market places, social media, and every place we can reach. Serving God is functioning as a vessel of God's love: receiving His love, loving Him, and loving men.

The concept of full-time ministry is the thinking that only ministers engaged in church or missionary service on a full-scale basis are full-time ministers. The truth is every believer is a full-time minister with varying scopes. All our work is a ministry because the primary purpose of working is to represent God.

The talents and gifts we have, the opportunities we get in life are for representing God. Whether it is sports, business, flying planes, farming, scientific research, or whatever engagement, it should be a way of serving God. Not something independent of God but a God-given opportunity. In that way, we will not have the often-dichotomous way of living, where a person is away from God at work till, he comes to seek God in the church meeting.

Presently, it is hard to see God in the market place; He is left behind on corporate matters of importance and later incorporated when we need Him. That is not the way we should live as sons of God. It is not the way we should do things. The believer must be conscious of God every moment, in sleep, in daily activities, in church, in every corner. Since God dwells in a believer's heart, how can He be presumed absent wherever the believer is.

Engaging in the fivefold ministry, e.g., pastor, the evangelist, is no easy task for sure, and it is not a place to get into unless you feel called and convicted to it. Some have got into it out of selfish ambitions and lack of other opportunities only to run away forsaking their flock. The one who gets into such ministry must be sure the Lord is leading him in a particular direction and must believe the Lord will sustain him all through. It is a journey of faith where a fainthearted cannot stand for long. For others engaged in various activities, every opportunity is for the sake of the kingdom.

The place of ministry is the dearest. It is the priority, the primary motivation. Every activity should be for serving God. As the Word says, *"Work willingly at whatever you do, as though you were working for the Lord rather than for people. Remember that the Lord will give you an inheritance as your reward and that the master you are serving is Christ. (Colossians 3:23-24)*

HOPE

'With hope, there is a better life. Without it, life loses value or meaning. Keep hope alive even if you can barely do it, it will prove worthwhile when the storm has passed.'

Hope is the expectation of coming good, an essential component of life that keeps one waiting and working despite discouragements and challenges. It is a state of mind that defies all odds to achieve a particular goal. Hope has a purpose, not a naïve feeling of false expectation.

Hope is the excellent ingredient of patience and endurance amid suffering and trials. The feeling that things will change for the better, even while it is dark. That light will come because there is a great God who changes circumstances.

There is hope in that our God has done all things for us in Jesus Christ, and no one who trusts in Him loses. The persistent challenge is confusion. We need always to tune our ears to hear clearly from God, to receive the divine knowledge that unlocks our timing for the fulfillment of our hope. Our hope as Christians goes beyond the issues of daily life and stretches into the eternity future.

We have the hope of salvation from the presence of sin, the hope of glory in Christ Jesus. To all who have accepted Christ, the promise of salvation has become real. We look at the future savings acts of God based on the redemption wrought in the past. If God gave His Son for our salvation, He would do everything for us in the future. There is hope in that the Spirit who raised Christ from the dead, the same Spirit now lives in us.

We have the assurance that the One who paid the highest price for our lives can provide anything we need. If He graciously gave His son to die for us, He can give anything else we need. Suffering is not sufficient to kill hope. Paul, writing to the Corinthians, says, *"we think you ought to know, dear brothers and sisters, about the trouble we went through in the province of Asia. We were crushed and overwhelmed beyond our ability to endure, and we thought we would never live through it. We expected to die. But as a result, we stopped relying on ourselves and learned to rely only on God, who raises the dead. And he did rescue us from mortal danger, and he will rescue us again. We have placed our confidence in him, and he will continue to rescue us." 2 Corinthians 1:8-10*

When our hope is Christ, living or dying for Him is satisfactory. Since death cannot separate us from Him, we get to a point where troubles no longer scare us. It is not a point of lethargy and giving up; it is the level of seeing things in the light of eternity. In such standards, God shows us His mighty power.

Perhaps nothing tests the reality of hope better than the certainty of death, rejection, or defeat. The threat of imminent death has a way of shaking up people to the real aspects of life. Some of the elements, like the value of life, its worth, impact, and length, have the potential of either spurring a great resolve or crushing desires for good. Rejection and failure have a way of gnawing at expectations and making a mock of life. But whatever you go through, whatever you face have hope of better things in Christ.

This world has enough troubles to keep us crying all the days of our lives. The reason the world is so severe a place is because it is a system of the enemy. The world system seeks to give supplies at the cost of one's life. But thanks to our Father, who nourishes us by His grace.

To retain hope in an unforgiving world, we must trust in God always that He knows everything and has made us understand all things. He has given us answers to issues that threaten our hope, and He is our Answer. In Him, we also minister answers to those who have lost confidence in the course of their lives, restoring life in full measure.

I have been without faith many times previously; being jobless, being sick, bereaved, failed several times, but I still hope in the Lord. He is so good we ought to trust Him, and this I do, I keep my hope alive. Hope for better things in Him, hope for Him.

EXCELLENCE

Throughout this book, we have studied various aspects, things to lay aside, practices to embrace, we have also examined several challenges in the path to excellence. With that sorted out, we can now get to the final stretch. *Excellence is not only a discipline but an anointing. The anointing of excellence flows into a believer who sits under the instruction and rebuke of a spiritual leader.* By following the instructions of the leader, a believer begins to operate in excellence. Perfection rises in place of mediocrity, ignorance, indifference, and negativity.

God's excellence

God has called us to excellence, to His way of doing things. No work of God throughout eternity has been mediocre. It is amazing how God loves an excellent job, and how He has manifested it through His creation and in dealings with man. The expanse of the universe with everything in it; the galaxies, the stars in their vast numbers, solar systems, planets, black holes, and objects without number in space. How all these bodies are in constant and orderly motion, the beauty of the Earth, and its fullness.

Adam made in God's image showing God's excellence in men's lives. In the book of Exodus, we see the perfection of God in anything He directs. The tabernacle design, the priests' dressing, the ephod, and the chest piece all made with great skill and care. The priest's garments were glorious and beautiful.

The Lord specifically chose Bezalel and Oholiab as the master craftsmen, filled them with His Spirit giving them great wisdom, ability, and expertise in all kinds of crafts. The order of sacrifice and worship was excellent too. We cannot help but marvel at the specifications of the Lord. It was nothing like what the Israelites knew. They had never seen such detailed skill and expertise before. The work of Egypt was nothing compared to these, neither the work of all the other kingdoms. God was birthing them into a new culture.

We also see the nature of the ministry of our Lord while on earth: so powerful and effective, wholesome and timely, efficient, and glorious. God's working in the first church, their order and function, how he used the apostles as master builders, and His continual ministry in the lives of believers throughout history tastes excellent. The most gratifying example of excellence is the Word of God, in the form, structure, layers of meaning, principles, and keys. The diversity of writing, revelations, grace, life, and fullness in the Word.

God's Desire and our State

Our Father loves excellence, and we cannot settle for any less. Yet our efforts often fall below par, clouded by character and personality flaws. The result becomes something dismal and unappealing to any wise man. Most of the attempts bear terrible short-sightedness and lack of grand vision. From the village, all the way to the highest offices in the world, we observe more cases of mediocrity than of excellent work ethic and thought. In the churches too, some of the service and activity earn ridicule from nonbelievers. Love for power, envy, and hypocrisy are characteristic of many gatherings in the nations.

How shall we break from this average, ordinary level and set forth acceptable standards? It should not be that we excel in matters, academic and professional, yet our beliefs and values are not any better. Or are faithful in church yet in our work we cannot seem to offer sound advice. A person of excellence will excel in every bit of life.

Our generation is living in times when the knowledge of God has increased than in earlier times. Yet, with all the experience available to us, we have not significantly thought enough. Few leaders have achieved anything close to what Joseph, David, Daniel, Joshua, Apostle Paul, and fellow workers of the time did millenniums ago. They were men who knew excellence, so great were their works that even today, we refer to their practices in learning.

The Way to Excel

An interesting thing to note is that what is regarded excellent in a local setting may be a common thing in higher circles. Excellence is not a fixed reference point but a divine nature that manifests in all circumstances. To pursue excellence and attain it, we must look at the Potter who made us and who continues to shape us in our daily living.

The way to excellence is a three-step process in *3 John 1:2, "dear friend, I hope all is well with you and that you are healthy in body as you are strong in spirit."* Excellence begins with the spirit when the inner man is well nourished in the Lord and enjoys communion with God. The next level is good health; health is the thing to be desired after the spirit's prosperity. In good health, the inner grace manifests in Christian service. Last is prospering in the material things and daily affairs. Note how the foundation is built from the spirit outwards and how each level builds up to the next.

Excellence is about the fullness of Christ manifested in our lives. Jesus Christ is excellent. As we sit under the instruction of His Word, we are receiving His Spirit of excellence in full measure. May you settle it in your mind to pursue excellence. Excellence demands constant improvement and readjustment, continually adopting new heavenly patterns. In heaven, all things are all always new.

"And they sang a new song with these words..." Revelation, 5:9.

"This wonderful choir sang a new song in front of the throne of God..." Revelation 14:3

If you are serving in ministry, you should desire excellence like that of the Lord Jesus while on earth. If it is leadership, be like Daniel, Nehemiah, David, Joseph, Paul, such men. If it is faith, excel in faith like Abraham. Excel in giving more than the Macedonian believers. Excel in doctrine and church building like Paul. Concerning war, and our fight is not physical but spiritual, excel more than Joshua and David. David is the man who never lost a battle because he had an army like the armies of heaven.

"Day after day, more men joined David until he had a great army, like the army of God." 1 Chronicles 12:22

"I have found David, my servant; with my sacred oil, I have anointed him. My hand will sustain him; surely, my arm will strengthen him. The enemy will not get the better of him; the wicked will not oppress him. I will crush his foes before him and strike down his adversaries" Psalms 89:20-23.

Today we have a better deal than David, that we are more than conquerors in Christ Jesus, we are people of victory!

I have observed that it is in places where people know Christ that true freedom exists. In such areas, women have the same dignity and contribution as men, and everyone has an equal opportunity for prosperity. Where men have a fear of the Lord in their hearts, there is excellence. There is in the hearts of those who fear the Lord repentance and a desire to honor God. This desire pushes them to excellence, as they will not do anything that does not glorify God.

Results

Pursuing excellence rewards richly. The fullness of Christ in a person manifests as continual growth in the grace of God, unbroken fellowship with the Holy Spirit, and fruitfulness in spiritual living. Fruitfulness is growth and multiplication in ministry, market place, and investments. God's fulness also involves victory over self, abounding in higher measures of love, and continual life of worship.

Excellence glorifies God. Pursuing excellence is seeking to be Christ-like. It is a way found pleasing before Him.

Wherever there is true excellence, there is wealth, both spiritual and material. Spiritual wealth includes grace and knowledge of God.

Excellence brings honor to a man. A man who excels gets favor from God and men.

Excellence brings dominion. As you distinguish yourself, you come into jurisdiction over environments and systems. Dominion is vested in the image of God in us, which image is Christ in us.

Misconceptions

In today's society, people confuse excellence with perfectionism, thus view it as unnecessary. But the distinction is more practical, more real than mere displeasure with the quality of things. Excellence relies on heavenly patterns, not human preferences.

Excellence is not in the chores we do. It is in being the firstborn son of God. If you are a son of God, you can do great things. Greatness is not in leadership positions.

Excellence is not to be confused with pride, selfish ambition, or the habits of consumerism. It is not about acquiring material things. It is about living above the ordinary. *"And now, dear brothers and sisters, one final thing. Fix your thoughts on what is true, and honorable, and right, and pure, and lovely, and admirable. Think about things that are excellent and worthy of praise." Philippians 4:8*

The Future

God is preparing a magnificent church, a standard that the entire world is coming to observe. Be part of the process.

"In the last days, the mountain of the LORD's house will be the highest of all- the most important place on earth. It will be raised above the other hills, and people from all over the world will stream there to worship. People from many nations will come and say, 'Come, let us go up to the mountain of the LORD, to the house of Jacob's God. There He will teach us His ways, and we will walk in His paths.' For the LORD's teaching will go out from Zion; His Word will go out from Jerusalem." Micah 4:1-2

The mountains of the earth mentioned in this passage are world systems of governance. These could include education systems, health systems, technology systems, transport systems, political systems, etc. They are popularly known as the seven mountains of influence, and they are all failing. Instead of trying to conquer falling mountains, go to the mountain that is rising in relevance. The church (Mount Zion) is rising higher and higher.

There is no better thing to do than to be part of the mountain of excellence, mount Zion, where excellence is a default setting in man.

EPILOGUE

We have taken a short journey examining our case and looking at the way to follow. I hope the insights shared have been of value to you. I hope you have taken the challenge and that you will help others along the way. Blessings.

About the Author

Joseph Kasonga is a graduate of Egerton University, Kenya, where he studied BSc. Natural Resource Management. He has worked in various sectors including environmental management, interior design and textiles, agriculture, freelance writing and he is also an author. Joseph ministers the gospel of the Lord Jesus Christ under Kingdom Glory Church, a ministry dedicated to restoring true worship as envisaged in the restoration of the tabernacle of David. Joseph expresses his passion for guiding the youth and those young at heart, through this profound message of following the heavenly patterns of excellence in daily living.

Milton Keynes UK
Ingram Content Group UK Ltd.
UKHW010933231123
433129UK00001B/79